THIS BOOK BELONGS TO: David Stewart

DATE STARTED:

PUBLISHED BY YM360

6-11-22

David, It has been a great week at camp and I'm so glad you came. I wanted to encourage you to keep asking questions as you continue developing your walk with Christ. This book will be a great resource for you and I hope you take the time to work through it daily. I'm always available for questions if you have them. I'm praying for you and for your relationship with Christ. Again I'm so glad you came this year and hope you come back again next year!

- Ryan Bender

David,

I'm so glad you came to camp this week! It has been an awesome week and I've enjoyed watching you jump into everything! I want to encourage you to continue seeking Jesus. Keep searching. Keep asking questions! Keeping leaning into Jesus and slowly letting go of everything else. He is worth pursuing and I pray this book helps you do that! I'm always here if you need me. I believe in you buddy! Love ya!

Philippians 1:6 Pastor J.C.

Published by YM360 in the United States of America.

ISBN: 9781954429116

[20] Now to him who is able to do **far more abundantly** than all that we ask or think, according to the power at work within us,

[21] **to him be glory** in the church and in Christ Jesus throughout all generations, **forever and ever.** Amen.

- Ephesians 3:20-21

CON

TABLE OF TENTS

WEEK 3

WEEK 4

GETTING STARTED

If you're reading this, the chances are good that sometime recently, you spent a few days going through *So Much More* with your youth group. Maybe you did this during a Disciple Now, a retreat, or at camp. Wherever you started your journey with *So Much More*, this book will help you continue it.

If we're honest, we can be guilty of getting so caught up with what's happening on the screen in our hands that it captures all our attention. We allow our lives to only be as big as the next most pressing decision. Our routines hold us captive. The problem is that this is a pretty shallow way to look at our life and our faith.

As humans, we can become nearsighted and forget that there is a God who is eternal. We get stuck in our routines and lose sight of God's plan for us and the world. It's too easy for us to miss the "way-more-than-we-could-possibly-imagine" future God has for us.

So Much More is all about showing you that it doesn't have to be this way. In this book, you're going to take a deeper look at the concepts in *So Much More*. Look at the next page to see how this book works.

HOW THIS BOOK WORKS

Here are a few things you need to know to put this book to good use.

Start With This Advice

Whether you're super-committed and read your Bible each day or struggle to read a few verses a couple of times a week, the key to sticking with this through four weeks is commitment. Your routine may change, but your commitment to meet God each day has to be there. Tell yourself that whether or not you read this journal at the same time each day, or if you read it whenever you get a few extra minutes, you'll make it a priority in your daily life.

Have Your Bible Open

Resist the urge to ignore the spots where this book will tell you to read a passage of Scripture. The close relationship with God that you want only happens by reading and doing what's in the Bible. Have it open as you go through this book.

Each Week Is Structured the Same, But Is Different

Each week's content works in similar ways. But each day is different. And there are a lot of different kinds of activities. Some will take 3-5 minutes, some 10-15. Some will ask you to look at two or three passages of Scripture; some will ask you to think about a concept. The variety will make it easier to stick with and help you learn in different ways that are suited to you.

What If I Miss A Day of Reading? Or Three?

Don't give up! Take this at your pace! The goal is for you to grow closer to God. If you miss a day or two (or four), don't throw in the towel. Pick this book back up and start where you left off. You can do this! And by doing it, you'll show the world that God makes an incredible difference in the lives of His followers. So, hang in there! You've got this!

Well, that's what you need to know to get started! Turn the page to read the introduction to Week 1.

Week 1 Intro

Before you start Week 1, read this short intro.

There is so much more to God than we could possibly imagine. That is the theme of *So Much More* and the theme of this first week.

God is more.

That's an interesting statement, isn't it? God is more. Period. He is simply ***MORE.***

God is more. He is more than us. More than any other. More than we can imagine. More than we could ever expect. He is more. And this thought should make us full of wonder and comfort.

Because God is more, He alone is worthy of our love and devotion.

You will spend the first few days of this journal reviewing the themes you covered in *So Much More*. And you'll re-discover that God is more wonderful, more powerful, and more loving than any of us can ever comprehend.

Are you ready to jump in?
Turn the page, and let's get started.

O MUCH MORE SO MUCH MORE SO M
CH MORE SO MUCH MORE SO MUCH

Read the passage below and answer the questions on the next page.

Begin this day's devotion by reading Ephesians 3:20-21. It's printed below, but if you have a Bible handy, consider reading it there.

Ephesians 3:20-21

[20] Now to him who is able to do far more abundantly than all that we ask or think, according to the power at work within us, [21] to him be glory in the church and in Christ Jesus throughout all generations, forever and ever. Amen.

Paul had a close relationship with the church in Ephesus. He had essentially started the church on his second missionary journey and kept a close friendship with them. This particular passage comes at the end of Paul's prayer for the Ephesians. He had prayed that they would be filled with the Holy Spirit and that they would understand the love God had for them.

Look back at how Paul described God in verse 20. The phrase "far more abundantly" is a powerful one. God can do abundantly more than we expect. That's pretty awesome. Abundant means overflowing. Abundant means more than we can hold or carry or grasp. But that's not what Paul said. Paul said God can do FAR MORE abundantly. That's like "abundant times abundant"! That's how awesome God is. He isn't just capable of more than we can expect or imagine; He's capable of SO MUCH MORE.

Questions to Consider

1. Paul wrote that God is "able to do far more abundantly than all that we ask or think." Be honest with yourself: what limitations do you put on God?

2. Think of a time recently when you had a need but weren't confident in God's ability to meet it. Why do you think we have this tendency?

3. Paul makes a really wild statement. He says that God can accomplish all these things according to the "power that is at work within us." Paul is talking about the Holy Spirit. How does it make you feel knowing you have the power of God inside you? How does this change your expectations of what God can do in and through you?

4. In verse 21, what does Paul say should be the result of God doing such great things in us and the world? What role do you play in giving God glory?

week **ONE** day **TWO**

Who is God to you? This is the question today's devotional will challenge you with.

Who is God to you?

If you recall the first day of *So Much More*, you got to see who God was to David. Take a moment and read 1 Chronicles 29:10–13. Remember, this is David praying aloud in front of his people. In his prayer, we see who God was to David.

Write down some of the words David used to describe God:

It is very clear from David's description of God that David knew God. David could say these things about God because He had experienced God in this way. Everything David said about God was true. They were characteristics that described God. David wasn't making stuff up. He was accurately describing God in a way that was true and right.

David essentially says that God is greater than anyone or anything in existence. God backs this up in His own words through the prophet Isaiah. Read Isaiah 55:8-9. How does God describe Himself in this passage? Write down your answer in the space below:

You're going to get the chance to do what David did. You're going to take some time to describe who God is to you and why.

In the space below, write a description of God in the left-hand column and explain why you know this to be true based on an experience you've had with God. Then, when you're done, spend some time praying to God, thanking Him for His greatness and majesty.

WHO GOD IS	HOW I KNOW

WEEK ONE DAY THREE

Read the following quote and respond to it on the next page.

One of the concepts you covered in *So Much More* is the so-much-more of God's love. God loves us more than we could possibly imagine. The depth of His love is so vast that we can't conceive of it. God's love for us changes everything about who we are. Read the quote below and take a few minutes to reflect on what it means to you.

"Trust God's love. His perfect love. Don't fear he will discover your past. He already has. Don't fear disappointing him in the future. He can show you the chapter in which you will. With perfect knowledge of the past and perfect vision of the future, he loves you perfectly in spite of both."

- Max Lucado

Questions to Consider

1. What do you think it means to "trust" God's love?

2. How is God's perfect love different from the love people have?

3. How does it make you feel that God loves you despite knowing everything about your past and future?

4. Spend some time in prayer and thanksgiving to God for His perfect, unfailing, so-much-more-than-you-can-imagine love.

WEEK 1
DAY 4

One of the truths you discovered in *So Much More* is that God's vision for your life is so much greater than you can anticipate. But it doesn't stop there. Not only does God have a plan for you, but He is also present with you as you go. This is a powerful truth that should fill you with hope.

When we consider the "so much more" of God, it can be overwhelming in a good way. But sometimes, we consider our own lives, and we are left somewhat underwhelmed. We look around us and ask, "Is this it? Is this all God has for me"? The wonderful news is that God's so much more doesn't just stop with Him. God has a vision for our lives that is WAY more than we can comprehend. His great desire is to use us, His people, to change the world for His sake.

The best news of all? He goes with us. He doesn't wind us up and set us free. He goes before us and prepares a way, then walks with us down the path He has directed. This is a POWERFUL message for you that will challenge and equip you to lean into what God has in store for you.

But just because God goes with us, it doesn't mean we won't be scared or uneasy about where we're headed. God addresses this in Isaiah 41:10.

Fear not, for I am with you; be not dismayed, for I am your God;
I will strengthen you,
I will help you, I will uphold you with my righteous right hand.
- Isaiah 41:10

Read that verse at the top of the page. Read it again if you need to.

Here's a question: Where in your life do you need strength?

Describe how you've gone to God to seek His strength in this area.

What basis does God give for you not being afraid?

What does God promise to do?

Spend a few minutes in prayer, seeking God's strength and comfort for the things in your life that cause you to be afraid. Trust that He is big enough to handle these.

Week One, Day 5

Read the prompt below and spend some time journaling your thoughts on the next page.

Read John 14:15-17.

[15] "If you love me, you will keep my commandments. [16] And I will ask the Father, and he will give you another Helper, to be with you forever, [17] even the Spirit of truth, whom the world cannot receive, because it neither sees him nor knows him. You know him, for he dwells with you and will be in you."

If you have been saved by faith in the work and person of Jesus, you have been given an incredible source of strength and power. You have been given the Holy Spirit to literally live inside of you. God Himself is with you all the time, giving you the strength to face everything life throws at you.

This truth reshapes how you see yourself, your life, the world around you, your future, etc. In short, it changes everything.

On the next page, spend some time writing down how this truth impacts your life. Think about how you feel God's presence each day. Think about what it means for you that God is always with you and that you are never alone. Think about your potential to impact the world around you just because God's Spirit is always with you. Write down your thoughts and spend some time in prayer.

WEEK ONE RECAP

This week was a time for us to lay the foundation for what you will be looking at the rest of the week.

This week you learned that God is able to do far more abundantly than all that you ask or think, according to the power at work within you. You learned that God is so much more than you can ever imagine, but out of His grace, makes Himself known to you. You learned that God's love is so much more complex and complete than you could ever expect. You learned that God's vision for your life is so much greater than you can anticipate and that He is present with you as you go. And you learned that God has given His people a source of strength that is so much more powerful than most ever realize.

It would be enough if this were all you learned in this book. But there is so much more coming your way.

Spend some time reflecting on what you learned this week. Maybe go back over a devotion that jumped out at you. Then, get ready for next week.

. . . even when we were dead in our trespasses,

God made us alive together with Christ

by grace you have been saved.

- Ephesians 2:5

Week 2 Intro

Before you start Week 2, read this short intro.

Who are you?

You could choose to answer that question in a variety of ways. You could talk about your family. You could list out your hobbies. You could even share where you live or where you were born. Any of these would be OK answers. But if you really want to paint a picture of who you are, you'd share your characteristics.

Are you funny? Are you smart? Are you quiet, or do you like to talk a lot? Are you athletic, musically inclined, or both? Are you trustworthy? Do you have a temper? What is your overall attitude? Each of these questions points to your characteristics. If you listed out your characteristics and handed them to someone, that person would have an excellent idea of exactly who you are.

We can approach God the same way. The Bible teaches us the characteristics of God, and by learning them, we can know who God is. That's what you're going to do this week: study some of the characteristics of God. After all, for us to believe that God is so much more than we can imagine, we have to start somewhere.

Turn the page, and let's learn about some of God's characteristics.

Read the passage below and answer the questions on the next page.

Eternal. Unchanging. Always existing.

These are a few words to describe the first characteristic of God you're going to be learning about. God is eternal. He always has been. He was never born and never created. He has always existed.

Read the passage below:

Isaiah 40:28

"Have you not known? Have you not heard? The LORD is the everlasting God, the Creator of the ends of the earth. He does not faint or grow weary; his understanding is unsearchable."

Isaiah says that God is everlasting. He is the Creator of all things. Therefore He came before all things. Isn't it great how Isaiah describes the result of God's eternal nature? He says that because God has always existed, He is incapable of growing tired or getting run down. He doesn't age. He never changes.

The reason this is such great news for the world and us is that God is always on watch. He never has to take a break. He never grows tired of engaging with us and with His creation. We can always count on Him to be present and active in our lives.

Questions to Consider:

1. We are the opposite of eternal, aren't we? How does this truth make God's desire to be in relationship with us even more meaningful?

2. What if God wasn't unchanging? What if He could not be counted upon to be who He is at all times? How would that change the way you related to God?

3. One of the gifts God gives us through the salvation He offers through His Son, Jesus, is eternal life. How does God's eternal nature allow Him to offer us this amazing gift?

week **TWO** day **TWO**

Read the passage below and work through what it means that God is omnipotent.

On the count of three, shout out the strongest person you know: One, two, three! I sincerely hope you were in a crowded place when you read this, and it caused people to look at you like a crazy person.

Here's the deal: that super strong person you pictured? They have nothing on God. As you learn about who God is this week, it would be a big mistake to skip over God's power. The word we use to describe God's power is a big one: omnipotent (pronounced "om-NIH-potent," with the emphasis on the second syllable.) It comes from two Latin words: "omni-," meaning "all," and "-potent," meaning "powerful." So when we say God is omnipotent, we're saying that He is all-powerful.

We see this truth communicated throughout the Bible. One verse where this aspect of God's character is clearly stated is in Deuteronomy 3:24:

"O Lord GOD, you have only begun to show your servant your greatness and your mighty hand. For what god is there in heaven or on earth who can do such works and mighty acts as yours?"

This is Moses speaking, and he asks what's called a rhetorical question. When he says, "what god is there in heaven or on earth who can do such works and mighty acts as yours," he's saying, "there is no one anywhere that is as powerful as God." God can do anything He sets out to do, and there is nothing He cannot do. Nothing can limit His power. He alone has this kind of power.

In Romans chapter 1, the Apostle Paul makes a really cool statement. He says this: "For what can be known about God is plain to [people], because God has shown it to them. For his invisible attributes, namely, his eternal power and divine nature, have been clearly perceived, ever since the creation of the world, in the things that have been made. So they are without excuse" (Romans 1:19–20). Paul says that no one can act like they don't think God exists because the evidence of His power is all around them in creation.

What about you?

Take a moment and think about four or five examples of where you see God's power on display in the world around you:

1. ______________________________
2. ______________________________
3. ______________________________
4. ______________________________
5. ______________________________

Now think about a few examples of times you have experienced God's power in your own life:

1. ______________________________
2. ______________________________
3. ______________________________
4. ______________________________
5. ______________________________

Think for a moment: How does God's omnipotence impact your relationship with Him?

Finally, spend some time in prayer praising God for His power and how He uses that power in the world and your life.

WEEK TWO DAY THREE

Read the verse below and spend some time writing down your thoughts in the space provided.

Ready for another "omni-" word today as you continue to learn about who God is? Good, because there's another one coming.

God is not only omnipotent, as you learned yesterday, but He is omniscient. Remember, "omni' means "all." The Latin root word that we get "-scient" from means "to know." Put them together, and you get "all-knowing." So, in addition to being all-powerful, God is all-knowing. That's a pretty amazing combination, isn't it?

God is all-powerful. There is nothing He can't do. He is also all-knowing. There is nothing He doesn't know. This isn't just about facts or knowledge. It's not just that God knows everything and would be a killer partner in a trivia contest (though He would). It's more about there being nothing that has ever happened or ever will happen that escapes God's knowing. No world event, no natural process, and no individual decision sneak past God's radar. If a flower blooms in the middle of a forest, God knows about it. If you think a thought in your bed at night before you sleep, God knows that thought. THAT'S what it looks like to be an all-knowing God.

In Romans 11:33, Paul expresses this truth in a worshipful way. You can almost hear his voice rise in praise to God. Paul says,

"Oh, the depth of the riches and wisdom and knowledge of God! How unsearchable are his judgments and how inscrutable his ways!"

Today, your task is to let your mind wander and simply ponder what it means to you that God is all-knowing. In our fast-paced, information-rich world, we don't do this enough. We don't stop and just consider God. So today, that is your challenge.

Spend time thinking about what it means to you that God is all-knowing. And write your thoughts below.

WEEK 2
DAY 4

Read the devotional below and answer the questions on the next page.

Today is the third day of learning about the "omni's" of God. You've learned that God is omnipotent (all-powerful) and omniscient (all-knowing). Today, you're going to learn that God is omnipresent.

Now, you don't need a degree in Latin to figure out the meaning of this one, do you? If you know by now that "omni" means "all," what do you think omnipresent means? That's right! God is all-present. His presence is not limited to one place. God isn't just hanging out in heaven until He's not. His presence is everywhere. Is your mind blown yet? Because it really should be.

God's ability to be everywhere at once is accomplished primarily through the Holy Spirit. Obviously, we know God doesn't have a physical body like we do and is therefore not limited to only being able to occupy a single place at any given time. Especially considering what we already know about His power (namely that He is SUPER powerful), it shouldn't be hard for us to believe that God is omnipresent.

Take a moment and read Psalm 139:7-12. This is a really beautiful expression of God's omnipresence. Verse 10 is sort of the culminating verse. It's the point where David says, "There is no place I can go where you are not." But the best thing about this verse is that it doesn't just say that God is everywhere; it says that BECAUSE God is everywhere, He can care for us ANYWHERE.

Questions to Consider:

1. How does God's omnipresence impact your faith? What does it mean that there is literally no place in creation where God isn't?

2. Think of the darkest time in your life. Now reflect on the fact that God was there with you. How does that change the way you see that time?

3. Have you ever felt like God wasn't with you? If God is omnipresent, and we know He is always with us, what does that mean about how you felt?

4. Spend some time in prayer today, thanking God that He is never not with you. Ask Him for the wisdom to understand this truth more and how it affects your life.

Week Two, Day 5

Read the devotional below and respond to the verses on the next page.

This is the last day this week that you will be learning about the characteristics of God. The mind-blowing thing is that the few days you have spent focusing on who God is doesn't even begin to scratch the surface. The Bible tells us about so many more of God's attributes that it would take weeks and weeks to learn them. And even then, just because you know the list of God's characteristics doesn't mean that you know ALL of who God is. God is so complex, so "other," so rich in His ways that we could study Him for the rest of our lives and still wouldn't fully know who He is. But if we could take a moment and try to look at one overarching characteristic, one description of God that might work as a suitable overview of the nature of who He is, we could do a lot worse than to focus on His goodness.

You see, God is good. He is perfectly, wonderfully good. There is nothing not good about Him. God is incapable of evil. He can't be bad or sinister in any way. Every motivation, every action, every aspect of God is 100%, completely, perfectly righteous. God is good.

You'll see two verses that speak to God's goodness on the next page. They are two of many in the Bible. Your goal today is to read those verses, reflect on them, and then make it a point in the next 24 hours to look for God's goodness in the world around you. When you encounter it, take note of it. Write it down on a note-taking app. Take a picture on your phone. Draw a word or a symbol on your hand or on a sticky-note that represents where you encountered God's goodness. Whatever you do, be more aware of God's goodness all around you today.

You are good and do good; teach me your statutes.

- Psalm 119:68

They shall pour forth the fame of your abundant goodness & shall sing aloud of your righteousness.

- Psalm 145:7

WEEK TWO RECAP

What an awesome week this was. This week you learned so much about God and His ways. You learned that God is eternal and unchanging. He always has been, and He always will be.

You learned that God is omnipotent. He is all-powerful, and nothing can keep Him from accomplishing what He wants to accomplish.

You learned that God is omniscient. He is all-knowing. Nothing happens without His knowledge. Nothing can slip by Him.

You learned that God is omnipresent. God's presence is everywhere. There is no place you can go where God isn't with you.

You learned that God is good. And what a wonderful truth that is. God is many things. But He is perfectly good in all His ways.

What a powerful week of learning about God's character and how it impacts the world and your life. Don't forget to think about these truths as you go throughout your day and your week. It's one way we grow closer to God.

Oh, the depth
of the riches
and wisdom and
knowledge of God!

How unsearchable
are his judgments
and how inscrutable
his ways!

- Romans 11:33

Week 3 Intro

You want your life to count for something, right? Most people do. Most people desire to look back over their lives and know they made a difference. You don't want to get to the end of the road and turn around only to find that the world isn't any different because you were in it.

Here's a coincidence: **God ALSO desires for your life to make an impact. A Kingdom impact.**

God has a plan for His Creation, and you are a part of that plan. God's vision for His people is to live on this earth experiencing God's goodness and to be messengers of this goodness to others. This is what it looks like to see God's Kingdom come to reality. Our lives are evidence to the world of the reality of a good God. And God has specific ways in mind for you to be a part of this.

This is what this week is all about: the so-much-more future God has in mind for you.

Turn the page and get started.

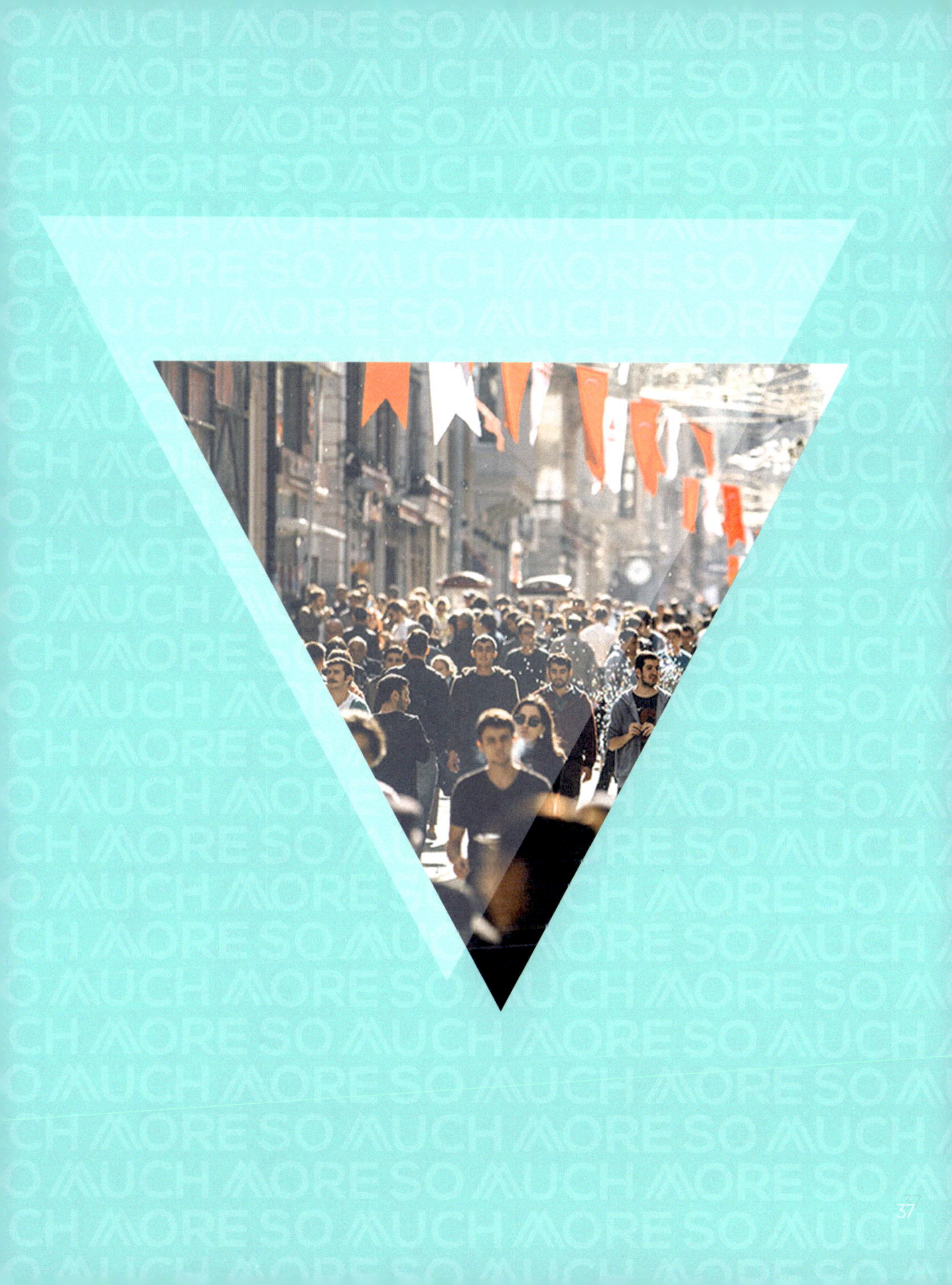
SO MUCH MORE SO MUCH MORE

Read the devotional below and answer the questions on the next page.

When you think about your future, what emotions come to mind? Do you feel uncertain or uneasy? Are you anxious about the next school year and what it will bring? Do you get overwhelmed about decisions like where or if you'll go to college? Do you wonder about your career or your vocation? Do you get nervous thinking about what will happen to your friendships in the next stage of your life? If you answered yes to any of these, don't worry. You're in good company.

A lot of teenagers worry about their future. But one of the things we must remember is that God does not. God knows exactly what's in store for you.

Take a second and read Ephesians 2:10. This verse comes at the end of an incredible description of what it looks like to come to saving faith in Jesus. Here at the end of this passage, Paul tells us one of the reasons God calls us to Himself: to show us all the good works God has prepared for us in our future.

There is this wonderful truth about the balance between God's sovereignty (His control over all things) and our freedom. The Bible tells us that we can decide how and what we will do in our lives. But because God is omniscient and eternal, He can see how our lives will play out. He knows the good we will choose before we choose it. And in that way, He has ordered our lives to be lives of goodness, meaning, and purpose, all for His glory. So when you think about your future, remember this: God has one planned for you that will bring joy to you and glory to Him. That should help with any anxiety you may have about your future.

Questions to Consider:

1. What aspects of your future give you the most anxiety?

2. How does knowing that God goes before you, and is with you, help you deal with those feelings?

3. As you make decisions about your future, what is your process for making sure they align with God's plan?

4. Spend some time in prayer, asking God to give you comfort about your future and to show you the direction He wants you to take.

week **THREE** day **TWO**

Read the prompts below, then reflect on the verse from page 41.

When it comes to our future, it can be hard to let go and trust God to lead us. And yet that is exactly what the Bible commands us to do.

Look at that verse over on page 41. Take a second and read it. What does it tell you to do? What does it say the result will be? Pretty straightforward, isn't it? And yet, too often, we overcomplicate the whole process.

Here's your challenge for today. Read that verse again. Then, think about what it means for your future. Start a conversation with God expressing to Him any aspects of this command that are hard for you. Think about what it means for you to apply this in your life. Then listen for what God has to say to you about where He wants to take you.

Trust in the Lord

with ALL your HEART,

and do not lean on your own understanding.
In all your ways acknowledge him,
and he will make straight your paths.

- Proverbs 3:5-6

WEEK THREE DAY THREE

Are you a planner? Some people are. Some people have a plan for what they are doing tomorrow, next week, and next year. Heck, some people probably even know where they want to be in five or ten years.

If you're not much of a planner, you may look at these people sometimes and just shake your head. You're more of a go-with-the-flow kind of person. You don't know what you'll be doing in five minutes, much less five years.

The interesting thing is that the Bible has a lot to say about this. Read James 4:13-16. If you're a planner, don't get stressed about this. James isn't saying that planning is bad. What he's doing is trying to teach us some perspective. James says that too many times, we act like we're in control of our futures. We can have a vision of where we want to be in the future, and there is nothing necessarily wrong with that. But James reminds us that we aren't in control of our lives! We're like a mist that comes and goes. Our plans don't add a single day to our lives.

So should we have plans for our future? Or should we just wing it? (I know some of you reading this would LOVE it if this were the case.) James gives us a clue in verse 15. Our attitude toward the future should be to seek God's direction for our lives and trust Him to lead us where He wants us, knowing that He is in control of all things.

It's a heart issue. Where is your hope, in you or God?

13 Come now, you who say, "Today or tomorrow we will go into such and such a town and spend a year there and trade and make a profit"— 14 yet you do not know what tomorrow will bring. What is your life? For you are a mist that appears for a little time and then vanishes. 15 Instead you ought to say, "If the Lord wills, we will live and do this or that." 16 As it is, you boast in your arrogance. All such boasting is evil.

James 4:13-16

Questions to Consider

1. How do you walk the line between making plans for your future and knowing that only God is in control?

2. If you were explaining with it looks like to someone else, how would you describe your process for seeing God's will about your future and being obedient to what He tells you?

3. What is it about these verses that should encourage you to live your life with a sense of urgency?

WEEK 3 DAY 4

Read the verse below and follow the prompts on the next page.

Many are the plans in the mind of a man, BUT it is the purpose of the Lord that will stand.

- Proverbs 19:21

Look at what Proverbs 19:21 says about your future. It says that we can make all sorts of plans. We can have all sorts of dreams. But only those that God wills to happen will last. But that doesn't mean we can't express our desires to God about what we want to do with our lives. It simply means that we must trust that some may fall in line with God's will and some may not.

Use this page to express to God where you'd like to see yourself in the future. In the space provided below, write a description of where you see yourself in five years. Make it as detailed as you want it to be.

Now, in the space below, write a prayer to God expressing your desire to do the things you just wrote. But tell God that you want nothing more than to do His will and that ultimately, you want to obey Him more than you want your wishes to come true.

Finally, close this time by writing a prayer of thanks to God for His unfailing love for you and His tender care over every aspect of your life.

Week Three, Day 5

Read the devotional below and write your thoughts in the space provided on the next page.

We've talked a lot about plans this week. Hopefully, you have seen loud and clear that God has a plan and that you have a role in it. God made you with your own interests, desires, dreams, and wants. This week, we've talked about how our role as God's children is to make sure that our plans align with His. That's the only way to a life of true joy.

Take a moment and read the verse below:

The heart of man plans his way, but the Lord establishes his steps. - Proverbs 16:9

There is a tendency in humans to read that verse and want to be a little territorial. We want to say, "Why can't I make plans in my heart? Why does God have to be the final say"? But here's the deal: God is the only one in the position to know if what we want is right and true or not. We should WANT God to establish, or approve, our steps. Why? Because His approval is all that matters. We can want what we want. But if it's not what God wants, we should be thankful that He is faithful to redirect us.

On the next page, spend some time reflecting on God's role in your future. Be honest with God about your feelings. Think about what it means to have God establish your plans.

WEEK THREE RECAP

What was your favorite part of learning about God's plan for your future this week?

Was it that God created you for good works in Christ?

Or maybe you enjoyed learning that you are called to trust in the Lord and not in your understanding of the future. Or maybe it was to appreciate the life God allows you because we truly don't control how long we will be allowed to live it.

Was it the idea that God's purpose for your future is the only lasting one?

Or maybe it was that you could take hope in God's power to establish your future and give your life assurance and purpose.

Whatever stood out to you this week, remember that the future is bright. God has a role for you to play, and the joy is watching and seeing what it is.

For we are his workmanship, created in Christ Jesus for good works, which God prepared beforehand, that we should walk in them.

- Ephesians 2:10

Week 4 Intro

Did you sleep with a blankie when you were little? Or an extra-special stuffed animal? OK, time to be honest: do you STILL sleep with one? It's OK to admit it. Lots of teenagers did (and in some cases still do). People grow up so fast in this world. There's nothing wrong with holding on to childhood a little longer.

Have you ever thought about why kids (and maybe you, lol) sleep with special blankets or stuffed animals? It's simple, really: there is comfort in their presence. The presence of a familiar object brings comfort to a small child (or a 17-year-old).

As we wrap up our last week in So Much More, we're going to focus on the so-much-more presence of God. God is with you as you go along on your journey. And it's a lot more than just comfort that He offers. ***So much more.***

You're about to learn all about God's presence with you and how it changes your life. Let's get started.

SO MUCH MORE

Read the devotional below and answer the questions on the next page.

Imagine that you were the most talented engineer ever. There was nothing you couldn't envision and then build. If you could dream it up in your head, you could make it come to life. Now imagine you were asked to build the perfect building. Money, size, and time were no object. Considering all of this, it would be safe to say that whatever building design you came up with would tell us everything we need to know about you and your idea of what makes the perfect building.

Pause for a second and read Genesis 1:26-31. This is the account of God making humans as part of Creation. Got it? Now read Genesis 3:8-13. This is the super-tragic moment that God encounters Adam and Eve after their sin against Him. We could spend a lot of time unpacking all the rich, theological truth in these two passages. But let's focus on something a little simpler.

There is something that these two passages have in common, but it's so subtle you might miss it at first. Here's a hint: look at Genesis 1:28 and Genesis 3:9 and find the word that is in both verses. Do you see it? It's the word "said." What both of these passages have in common is that they both depict God, the Creator, personally speaking with His creation. This is kind of a big deal. In fact, it might be bigger than you think. And it goes back to the intro to this devotional.

Like the engineer and the perfect building, we can learn about God by observing what He created. When God had a blank slate and created everything just like He liked it, before creation was ravaged by the effects of sin, He planned to personally be with humankind. Until sin broke their relationship, God walked in the Garden with Adam and Eve. He talked with them. His presence was with them. That was His intent for how we would be in relationship with Him. Of course, sin changed that. But knowing what God's original intent was for Him and us is a game-changer.

Questions to Consider:

1. This is a crazy way to think because you can't undo the past, but have you ever imagined what life would be like had Adam and Eve never sinned? What if God was still physically present with us? What would that be like?

2. What would you do if God were physically with you now in person? How would you act? What would you say?

3. Once we really think about God's plan to be present daily with His people, it hits home how destructive Adam and Eve's sin was. Sin created instant distance between God and humans that was never intended to be there. Can you think of how you experience the separation that sin causes between God and you?

4. Spend some time in prayer thanking God for His desire to be present in the lives of His children.

week **FOUR** day **TWO**

Read the devotional below and answer the questions on the next page.

This week's devotionals build directly on yesterday. So if you missed yesterday's (hey, it happens), maybe you should go back now and catch up.

This last week of *So Much More* is all about God's presence with us. Yesterday you learned that God's original plan for creation was for Him to be physically present with us, His children. Sin changed that. Adam and Eve's sin created a barrier between them and God. They were thrown out of the Garden of Eden because of their rebellion. And from that moment until now, with a few notable exceptions, the main way God's presence has been with His people has not been physical. As you learned in Week 2, Day 4's devotional, God is still present with us, but it's MAINLY through His Spirit.

There have been exceptions, of course. Read John 1:1-14. Verses 1-5 describe Jesus as "the Word." John tells us that Jesus is God and was present at Creation (along with the Father and the Spirit). That's all extremely awesome and connects with yesterday's devotional. But check out verse 14. What did the Word, Jesus, do? He became flesh. Jesus stepped out of heaven and became human while retaining His nature as God. Fully God, fully man, Jesus walked our earth. When He was grown, He began teaching and healing and performing miracles. In an incredibly powerful way, He showed us a glimpse of what it was like to be physically present with God. And it changed EVERYTHING.

Jesus came for sinners, to make a relational bridge back to God so that ANYONE who believed in Him would never be separated from God by sin again. Through His perfect life, sacrificial death on the cross, and miraculous resurrection, Jesus radically changed the nature of our relationship with God's presence. As we think about God's presence this week, Jesus' coming is the turning point in the conversation.

Questions to Consider:

1. Think about what you know about the Gospel and what Jesus came to do. In your own words, what do Jesus' life, death, and resurrection have to do with God's presence in your life?

2. If you could put yourself in the shoes of the men and women who got to hear and see Jesus, what do you think it meant to them that God had come down in their midst to walk and talk to them?

3. One thing we know about Jesus is that He didn't just come to earth to hang out and observe. He was intimately involved in the lives of the people He encountered. He healed the sick, comforted the lonely and the outcast, and preached the goodness of God's Kingdom. What does that mean to you today as you follow Christ?

WEEK FOUR DAY THREE

Read the devotional below and answer the questions on the next page.

In the last two days, you've learned about God's original intent for how His children would experience His presence. In the Garden of Eden, He walked and talked with Adam and Eve, which is mind-blowingly cool. But Adam and Eve rebelled against God, and it caused a break in their relationship that impacts us still today. God could no longer be in their presence physically because of their sin.

Yesterday you read about Jesus coming to earth as a man in the most radical expression of God's presence with us up to that time. In the Old Testament book of Isaiah, Jesus' coming was predicted hundreds of years before His birth. The prophet used the name Immanuel to describe Jesus because Immanuel means "God with us." But we know that Jesus didn't stay on earth forever. Three years after His public ministry began, He was crucified and buried. Miraculously, three days later, He arose from the dead. But even then, He didn't stay. He ascended into heaven, where He is to this day.

So, where does that leave us with God's presence? We're going to get into that a lot more tomorrow, but for today, let's paint a picture of the end of things. We've already looked at how the beginning went. How about the end?

Read Revelation 21:1-5. This is the end of the way things are and the beginning of how things will be. This is what we have to look forward to. One day, God will finally put an end to this sinful, broken world. And when He does, don't miss what He says about this new state of things: "Behold, the dwelling place of God is with man. He will dwell with them, and they will be his people, and God himself will be with them as their God" (Revelation 21:3). There will come a day when God returns things to the way He always intended them. This time, it will be forever.

Questions to Consider

1. On page 53, you were asked, "This is a crazy way to think because you can't undo the past, but have you ever imagined what life would be like had Adam and Eve never sinned? What if God was still physically present with us? What would that be like?" In Revelation 21, God answers that question for Himself. There is a future coming where all will be set right. When you think about the world and the impact of sin and evil on every aspect of our lives, how does knowing the future God has in store for us give you hope?

2. This future is only for those who have been saved by faith in Jesus and adopted into the family of God. How does this fact motivate you to share your faith with others who don't know Jesus?

3. How often do you think about heaven and eternity with God? The Bible says that we should think about it because it motivates us to live our lives to the fullest here. Maybe spend some time today thinking about what it will be like to be with God forever. Pray to God, praising Him that He has made a way for us to be with Him, personally, forever.

WEEK 4
DAY 4

Read the devotional below and answer the questions on the next page.

Normally, this would be the space to talk about the Holy Spirit's presence in our lives. After all, part of why the Holy Spirit was given to us is as a way of God telling us, "One day we'll be together forever. Until then, I'm giving you my Spirit to be present with you." We already looked at the Spirit's role in Week 1, Day 4's devotional. It wouldn't be a bad idea if you want to flip back and reread that. But we will do a little something different the last two days of this devotional and look at what impact God's presence with you has on your daily life.

Read Matthew 28:16-20. This is known as the Great Commission. A commission is a task or a job given to someone. When you know that definition, it makes this passage make sense. Jesus is tasking His disciples and, by extension, us, as His messengers to take the Gospel to every corner of the world. This is a big task that we don't have time to unpack in this space. But for our purposes, let's focus on the end of verse 20.

Jesus gives His disciples a tall task. But then He tells them that He will be with them as they go. This is a powerful truth of God's presence: God expects us to partner with Him in His rescue mission, and He empowers us to do so. He doesn't call us and leave us. He doesn't give us an assignment and then walk away. He says, "I want your help, and I will be present with you as you help me."

This promise of presence should change how we see ourselves and our faith. Let's spend a few minutes thinking about this a little more in-depth.

Questions to Consider

1. Have you ever had moments where sharing your faith was difficult? Describe how it made you feel.

2. What difference does it make that God is with you in these moments? Does it change anything that you're not alone?

3. If you worry about your effectiveness at sharing your faith with others, how does this change that? It's not only that God is with you; it's that He's authorized you to be His mouthpiece. How does this give you the confidence to be bold in expressing your commitment to God?

Week Four, Day 5

Read the words below and spend some time reflecting on the verse on the next page.

God's presence isn't just a fact; it's a promise. A promise of comfort. An assurance of peace and confidence. Look at the words of David in Psalm 23 on the next page. Here, David sees God as the Shepherd, walking His "flock" through the ups and downs of life. See what David says here about what happens when we walk through life's valleys. What does the shepherd do? He protects His sheep. His presence, even in the midst of danger, comforts them.

God's presence in our lives gives us peace. Are you at peace? Can you find comfort in God's presence even in the shadow of dark times? Read the words of Psalm 23:4 and allow them to speak to your heart. Take comfort in God's hand over your life. His presence goes with you.

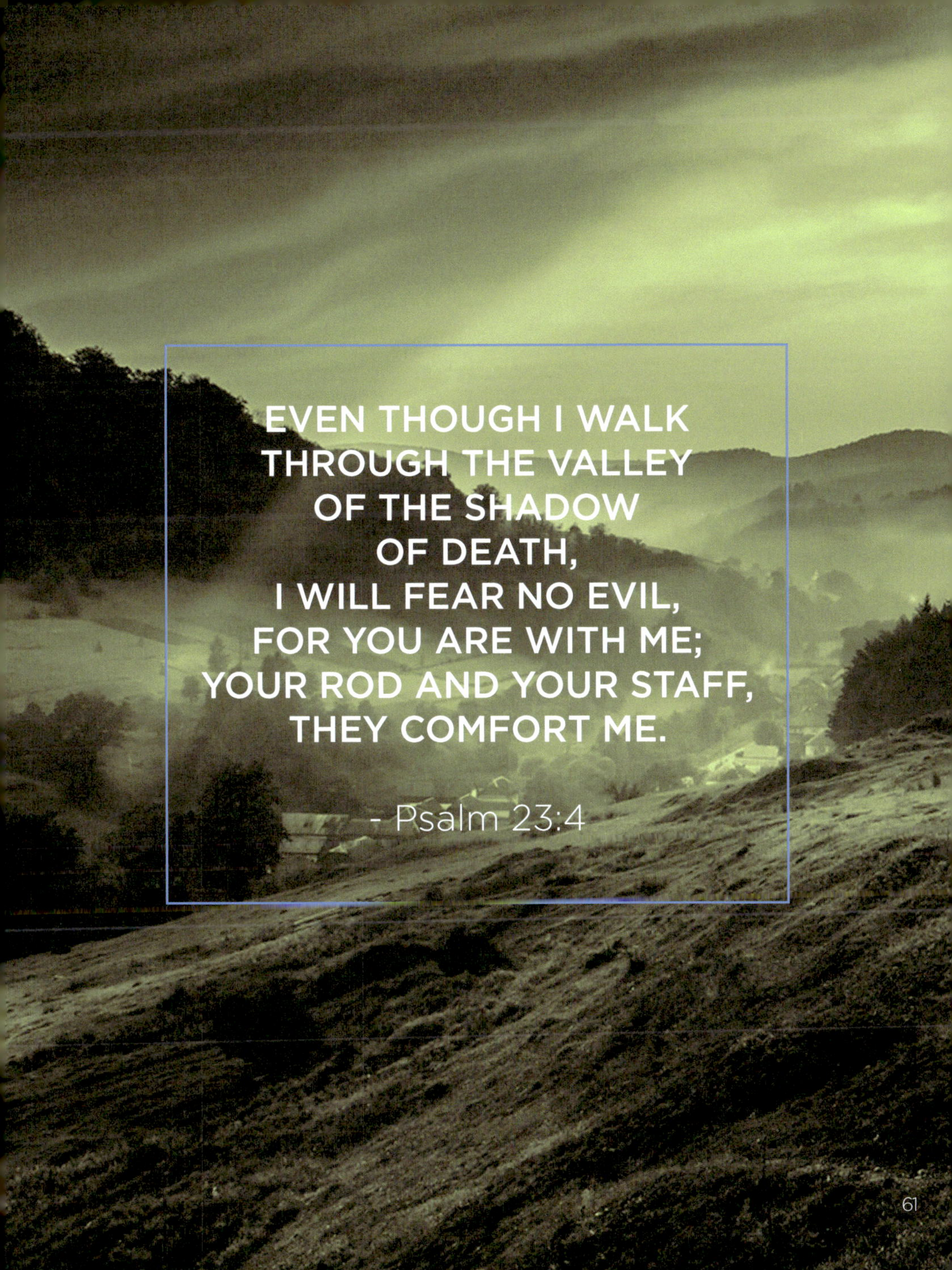
EVEN THOUGH I WALK
THROUGH THE VALLEY
OF THE SHADOW
OF DEATH,
I WILL FEAR NO EVIL,
FOR YOU ARE WITH ME;
YOUR ROD AND YOUR STAFF,
THEY COMFORT ME.
- Psalm 23:4

WEEK FOUR RECAP

This week was about God's presence. And the hope is that what you saw in HOW He is present is the same thing you saw in every other aspect we looked at. The nature of God's character, His plans, and His presence all go far beyond what we can imagine or expect.

Simply put, there is so much more to God. Period.

God never ceases to amaze and inspire in every way, in every interaction, in every glimpse we see of Him. And yet He loves us in such a personal, intimate way. Maybe you were able to take that from this book, as well.

As you move on from this journal, remember that God expects you to grow in your wisdom and knowledge of Him and be transformed by that knowledge. So take what you have learned and build on it. Allow God to use you. And don't be surprised that where He will take is you so much more than you could have planned yourself.

[20] Now to him who is able to do
far more abundantly than all that
we ask or think, according to the
power at work within us,

[21] **to him be glory** in the church
and in Christ Jesus throughout
all generations, **forever and ever.**
Amen.

- Ephesians 3:20-21

ABOUT THE AUTHOR

ANDY BLANKS

Andy Blanks is the Publisher and Co-Founder of YM360. A former Marine, Andy has been doing ministry since the early 2000s, mostly in youth ministry. During that time, Andy has led the development of some of the most popular Bible study curriculum and discipleship resources in the country. He has authored numerous books, Bible studies, and articles, and regularly speaks at events and conferences, both for adults and teenagers. He is active in his local church, teaching youth, adult, and men's small groups regularly.

Andy and his wife, Brendt, were married in 2000 and have lived in Birmingham, AL, ever since. They have four children, three girls, and one boy.

Graphic Design:
Fund the Nations

Page Layout:
Upper Air Creative

IF YOU'VE EVER STRUGGLED TO READ THE BIBLE, WE'VE GOT GREAT NEWS.

If we're honest, most of us find times where our passion for reading the Bible is just sort of missing. God feels far away. The Bible feels intimidating. It doesn't have to be that way.

"Wake Up: Rediscovering a Passion for God and the Bible" is a 31-day devotional designed to help you meet God in the Bible in ways you never have. And in doing so, your passion for God will be rekindled. Remember, God is always near. He is never far away. Sometimes, we simply need to know how to look for Him.

TO SAMPLE OR FOR ORDERING INFO,
GO TO YM360.COM/WAKEUP

A 3-PART DEVOTIONAL EXPERIENCE

DESIGNED TO HELP YOU BECOME A DISCIPLE OF CHRIST. IN A WORD, TO KNOW GOD AND MAKE HIM KNOWN.

The *New/Next/Now* Discipleship Bundle provides three powerful devotional experiences to help you grow from a new believer to an authentic disciple of Christ.

NEW: FIRST STEPS FOR NEW CHRIST-FOLLOWERS

One of the most used new believer resources in youth ministry, this powerful 4-week devotional experience will help new believers get off to a strong start on their new journey with Christ.

NEXT: GROWING A FAITH THAT LASTS

4-week devotional will help you take ownership of your faith. NEXT will teach: Why it's important to own your faith, What life's purpose has to do with God's mission, How to build spiritual habits that last a lifetime, and How to use the influence you already have for Christ.

NOW: IMPACTING YOUR WORLD FOR CHRIST (RIGHT NOW!)

You have the amazing potential to impact your world for Christ, not just some time in the future ... but right NOW! Today. Your world is rich with opportunities to share the hopeful message of the Gospel, and to show people the amazing difference Christ can make in their lives. Now will help you make the most of these opportunities!

TO VIEW SAMPLES OF *NEW, NEXT & NOW*
AND TO ORDER, GO TO YM360.COM/DEVOBUNDLE